The Catholic Children's Prayer Book

Belongs to: _Aurora Himmelspach_

Given by: _St. Joseph School_

Date: _4-1-2020_

Jesus said, "Let the children come to me and do not stop them, because the Kingdom of heaven belongs to such as these."

—Matthew 19:14

My Faith Journey

Date of Baptism: _____

Date of First Reconciliation: _____

Date of First Eucharist: _____

D1314369

saint mary's press

The rest of the prayers and practices contained herein have been verified against authoritative sources.

During this book's preparation, all citations, facts, figures, names, addresses, telephone numbers, Internet URLs, and other pieces of information cited within were verified for accuracy. The authors and Saint Mary's Press staff have made every attempt to reference current and valid sources, but we cannot guarantee the content of any source, and we are not responsible for any changes that may have occurred since our verification. If you find an error in, or have a question or concern about, any of the information or sources listed within, please contact Saint Mary's Press.

The content for this resource was acquired, developed, and reviewed by the content engagement team at Saint Mary's Press. Content design and manufacturing were coordinated by the passionate team of creatives at Saint Mary's Press.

Cover illustration and interior illustration by Nathan Hale.

Printed in the United States of America

4414 (PO6406)

ISBN 978-1-59982-788-9

The Catholic Children's Prayer Book

Everyday Prayers and Practices

Rosary Prayers

Introduction

There is an old church song that begins with the line "What a friend we have in Jesus," and it is true. God loves each one of us and wants nothing more than to be our lifelong friend.

Prayer is our way of talking to God. In prayer, we tell God what we need, we tell God we love him, and we ask God to be with us in everything we do. Sometimes we talk to God quietly in our hearts, and we know that God hears us. Other times, we talk to God using words other people have written. Those people know and love God and want us to know and love him as well.

In this book, you will find prayers to deepen your friendship with God. These prayers will help you talk to God and help you find ways during the day to stop, just for a minute, and offer a prayer. The prayers in this book will also help you talk to God as part of the Church, as you pray the prayers of the Mass and the Rosary.

Praying every day helps you realize how much God loves you, and it also helps you love God. As you come to know God more and more through prayer, you will grow in your love for him. We hope these prayers help you do that.

SIGN OF THE CROSS

In the name of the Father,
and of the Son,
and of the Holy Spirit. Amen.

GREETING

Priest: The Lord be with you.
Assembly: And with your spirit.

PENITENTIAL ACT, FORM A

I confess to almighty God
and to you, my brothers and sisters,
that I have greatly sinned,
in my thoughts and in my words,
in what I have done and in what I have
    failed to do,
through my fault, through my fault,
through my most grievous fault;
therefore I ask blessed Mary ever-Virgin,
all the Angels and Saints,
and you, my brothers and sisters,
to pray for me to the Lord our God.

🍃 PENITENTIAL ACT, FORM B

Priest: Have mercy on us, O Lord.
Assembly: For we have sinned against you.
Priest: Show us, O Lord, your mercy.
Assembly: And grant us your salvation.

GLORIA

Glory to God in the highest,
and on earth peace to people of good will.

We praise you,
we bless you,
we adore you,
we glorify you,
we give you thanks for your great glory,
Lord God, heavenly King,
O God, almighty Father.
Lord Jesus Christ, Only Begotten Son,
Lord God, Lamb of God, Son of the Father,
you take away the sins of the world,
    have mercy on us;
you take away the sins of the world,
    receive our prayer;
you are seated at the right hand of the Father,
    have mercy on us.

For you alone are the Holy One,
you alone are the Lord,
you alone are the Most High,
Jesus Christ,
with the Holy Spirit,
in the glory of God the Father.
    Amen.

RESPONSES TO THE READINGS

First and Second Reading
(at Conclusion)

Reader: The word of the Lord.
Assembly: Thanks be to God.

Gospel
(at Introduction)

Deacon or Priest: The Lord be with you.
Assembly: And with your spirit.
Deacon or Priest: A reading from the holy Gospel according to N [name of Gospel writer].
Assembly: Glory to you, O Lord.

Gospel
(at Conclusion)

Deacon or Priest: The Gospel of the Lord.
Assembly: Praise to you, Lord Jesus Christ.

NICENE CREED
(Nicene-Constantinopolitan Creed)

I believe in one God,
the Father almighty,
maker of heaven and earth,
of all things visible and invisible.

I believe in one Lord, Jesus Christ,
the Only Begotten Son of God,
born of the Father before all ages.
God from God, Light from Light,
true God from true God,
begotten, not made, consubstantial
    with the Father;
through him all things were made.
For us men and for our salvation
he came down from heaven,
and by the Holy Spirit was incarnate
    of the Virgin Mary,
and became man.

For our sake he was crucified under
    Pontius Pilate,
he suffered death and was buried,
and rose again on the third day
in accordance with the Scriptures.
He ascended into heaven
and is seated at the right hand of the Father.
He will come again in glory
to judge the living and the dead
and his kingdom will have no end.

I believe in the Holy Spirit, the Lord,
    the giver of life,
who proceeds from the Father and the Son,
who with the Father and the Son is adored
    and glorified,
who has spoken through the prophets.

I believe in one, holy, catholic and
    apostolic Church.
I confess one Baptism for the forgiveness
    of sins
and I look forward to the resurrection
    of the dead
and the life of the world to come.
Amen.

PRAYER OVER THE GIFTS

Assembly: May the Lord accept the sacrifice
at your hands
for the praise and glory of his name,
for our good
and the good of all his holy Church.

PREFACE

Priest: The Lord be with you.
Assembly: And with your spirit.
Priest: Lift up your hearts.
Assembly: We lift them up to the Lord.
Priest: Let us give thanks to the Lord our God.
Assembly: It is right and just.

HOLY, HOLY, HOLY
(Preface Acclamation)

Assembly: Holy, Holy, Holy Lord
  God of hosts.
Heaven and earth are full of your glory.
Hosanna in the highest.
Blessed is he who comes in the name of
  the Lord.
Hosanna in the highest.

MYSTERY OF FAITH

Priest: The mystery of faith.
Assembly (a): We proclaim your Death,
O Lord,
and profess your Resurrection
until you come again.

(or b): When we eat this Bread and drink
this Cup,
we proclaim your Death, O Lord,
until you come again.

(or c): Save us, Savior of the world,
for by your Cross and Resurrection
you have set us free.

THE OUR FATHER
(Lord's Prayer)

Our Father, who art in heaven,
hallowed be thy name.
Thy kingdom come;
thy will be done
on earth as it is in heaven.
Give us this day our daily bread;
and forgive us our trespasses
as we forgive those
who trespass against us;
and lead us not into temptation,
but deliver us from evil. Amen.

LAMB OF GOD
(Litany at the Fraction Rite)

Assembly: Lamb of God,
you take away the sins of the world,
have mercy on us.
Lamb of God, you take away the sins of
the world,
have mercy on us.
Lamb of God, you take away the sins of
the world,
grant us peace.

INVITATION TO COMMUNION

Priest: Behold the Lamb of God,
behold him who takes away the sins of the
world.
Blessed are those called to the supper of
the Lamb.
Assembly: Lord, I am not worthy
that you should enter under my roof,
but only say the word
and my soul shall be healed.

SENDING FORTH

Deacon, or Priest (a): Go forth, the Mass
is ended.
(or b): Go and announce the Gospel of the
Lord.
(or c): Go in peace, glorifying the Lord by
your life.
(or d): Go in peace.
Assembly: Thanks be to God.

GRACE BEFORE AND AFTER MEALS

Grace before Meals

Bless us, O Lord, and these your gifts,
which we are about to receive
   from your bounty,
through Christ our Lord. Amen.

Grace after Meals

We give you thanks, almighty God,
for these and all your gifts,
which we have received
   through Christ our Lord. Amen.

MORNING AND EVENING PRAYERS

Morning Prayer

O my God, I offer you this day,
all I do and think and say.
In union with what was done,
on earth by Jesus Christ,
your Son.
Amen.

Evening Prayer

God, our Father, this day is done.
We ask you and Jesus Christ, your Son,
that with the Spirit, our welcome guest,
you guard our sleep and bless our rest.
Amen.

ANGEL OF GOD

Angel of God, my guardian dear,
to whom God's love commits me here,
ever this day be at my side,
to light and guard, to rule and guide. Amen.

ACT OF FAITH

O my God, I firmly believe that you are one God in three Divine Persons, Father, Son, and Holy Spirit. I believe that your divine Son became man and died for our sins and that he will come to judge the living and the dead. I believe these and all the truths which the Holy Catholic Church teaches because you have revealed them who are eternal truth and wisdom, who can neither deceive nor be deceived. In this faith I intend to live and die. Amen.

ACT OF HOPE

O Lord God, I hope by your grace for the pardon of all my sins, and after life here to gain eternal happiness because you have promised it, who are infinitely powerful, faithful, kind, and merciful. In this hope I intend to live and die. Amen.

ACT OF LOVE

O Lord God, I love you above all things and I love my neighbor for your sake because you are the highest, infinite, and perfect good, worthy of all my love. In this love I intend to live and die. Amen.

PRAYER OF SAINT FRANCIS OF ASSISI

(Peace Prayer of Saint Francis)

Lord, make me an instrument of your peace.
Where there is hatred, let me sow love;
where there is injury, pardon;
where there is doubt, faith;
where there is despair, hope;
where there is darkness, light;
where there is sadness, joy.
O Divine Master, grant that I may not so much
    seek to be consoled as to console;
to be understood as to understand;
to be loved as to love.
For it is in giving that we receive;
it is in pardoning that we are pardoned;
and it is in dying that we are born to eternal life.
    Amen.

A PRAYER TO JESUS
(by Saint Richard of Chichester)

O most merciful Redeemer, Friend, and Brother,
May I know you more clearly,
Love you more dearly,
And follow you more nearly,
For ever and ever. Amen.

THE BEATITUDES

Blessed are the poor in spirit, for theirs is the Kingdom of heaven.

Blessed are they who mourn, for they will be comforted.

Blessed are the meek, for they will inherit the land.

Blessed are they who hunger and thirst for righteousness, for they will be satisfied.

Blessed are the merciful, for they will be shown mercy.

Blessed are the clean of heart, for they will see God.

Blessed are the peacemakers, for they will be called children of God.

Blessed are they who are persecuted for the sake of righteousness, for theirs is the kingdom of heaven.

(Based on Matthew 5:3–10. For more on the Beatitudes, see Matthew, chapters 5–7, and Luke, chapter 6, in *The Catholic Children's Bible*.)

THE TEN COMMANDMENTS

1. I am the Lord your God, you shall not have other gods before me.
2. You shall not take the name of the Lord your God in vain.
3. Remember to keep holy the Lord's Day.
4. Honor your father and your mother.
5. You shall not kill.
6. You shall not commit adultery.

7. You shall not steal.

8. You shall not bear false witness against your neighbor.

9. You shall not covet your neighbor's wife.

10. You shall not covet your neighbor's possessions.

(Based on Exodus 20:1–17. For more on the Ten Commandments, see Exodus, chapter 20, in *The Catholic Children's Bible*, or see the *Moses and the Ten Commandments Big Book*.)

WORKS OF MERCY

Corporal Works of Mercy

1. Feed the hungry.
2. Give drink to the thirsty.
3. Clothe the naked.
4. Shelter the homeless.
5. Visit the sick.
6. Visit the imprisoned.
7. Bury the dead.

Spiritual Works of Mercy

1. Counsel the doubtful.
2. Teach the ignorant.
3. Help the sinner.
4. Comfort the afflicted.
5. Forgive injuries.
6. Bear wrongs patiently.
7. Pray for the living and the dead.

SEVEN SACRAMENTS

1. Baptism
2. Confirmation
3. Holy Eucharist
4. Penance and Reconciliation
5. Anointing of the Sick
6. Holy Orders
7. Matrimony

ACT OF CONTRITION

My God,
I am sorry for my sins with all my heart.
In choosing to do wrong
and failing to do good,
I have sinned against you
whom I should love above all things.
I firmly intend, with your help,
to do penance,
to sin no more,
and to avoid whatever leads me to sin.
Our Savior Jesus Christ
suffered and died for us.
In his name, my God, have mercy. Amen.

THE HOLY DAYS OF OBLIGATION

Solemnity of Mary, Mother of God (January 1)

Ascension (40 days from Easter Sunday; may be celebrated on the last Thursday or Sunday before Pentecost)

Assumption of Mary (August 15)

All Saints' Day (November 1)

Immaculate Conception (December 8)

Christmas (December 25)

THE PRECEPTS OF THE CHURCH

1. Participate in Mass on Sundays and holy days of obligation. Keep these days holy. Avoid unnecessary work.

2. Confess your sins in the Sacrament of Penance and Reconciliation at least once each year.

3. Receive Holy Communion at least once a year, during the Easter season.

4. Follow the rules of fasting and abstaining from meat on the special days of Ash Wednesday, Good Friday, and the Fridays of Lent.

5. Give what you can to help meet the needs of the Church.

STATIONS OF THE CROSS

1. Jesus is condemned to death.
2. Jesus takes up his cross.
3. Jesus falls the first time.
4. Jesus meets his mother.
5. Simon helps Jesus carry the cross.
6. Veronica wipes the face of Jesus.
7. Jesus falls the second time.
8. Jesus meets the women of Jerusalem.
9. Jesus falls the third time.
10. Jesus is stripped of his garments.
11. Jesus is nailed to the cross.
12. Jesus dies on the cross.
13. Jesus is taken down from the cross.
14. Jesus is laid in the tomb.

SIGN OF THE CROSS

In the name of the Father,
and of the Son,
and of the Holy Spirit. Amen.

APOSTLES' CREED

I believe in God,
the Father almighty,
Creator of heaven and earth,
and in Jesus Christ, his only Son,
our Lord,
who was conceived by the Holy Spirit,
born of the Virgin Mary,
suffered under Pontius Pilate,
was crucified, died and was buried;
he descended into hell;
on the third day he rose again from the dead;
he ascended into heaven,
and is seated at the right hand of God the
    Father almighty;
from there he will come to judge the living
    and the dead.

I believe in the Holy Spirit,
the holy catholic Church,
the communion of saints,
the forgiveness of sins,
the resurrection of the body,
and life everlasting.
Amen.

THE OUR FATHER
(Lord's Prayer)

Our Father, who art in heaven,
hallowed be thy name.
Thy kingdom come;
thy will be done
on earth as it is in heaven.
Give us this day our daily bread;
and forgive us our trespasses
as we forgive those
who trespass against us;
and lead us not into temptation,
but deliver us from evil. Amen.

HAIL MARY

Hail Mary, full of grace,
the Lord is with thee.
Blessed art thou among women,
and blessed is the fruit of thy
    womb, Jesus.
Holy Mary, Mother of God,
    pray for us sinners,
now and at the hour of our death.
    Amen.

GLORY BE

Glory be to the Father,
and to the Son,
and to the Holy Spirit.
As it was in the beginning,
is now,
and will be forever. Amen.

FATIMA PRAYER

O my Jesus,
forgive us our sins,
save us from the fires of hell,
lead all souls to heaven,
especially those in most need of your mercy.
Amen.

HAIL, HOLY QUEEN

Hail, Holy Queen, Mother of mercy,
  our life, our sweetness and our hope.
To you do we cry, poor banished
  children of Eve.
To you do we send up our sighs,
  mourning and weeping in this valley of tears.
Turn then, most gracious advocate,
  your eyes of mercy toward us,
  and after this exile show to us the blessed
  fruit of your womb, Jesus.
O clement, O loving,
O sweet Virgin Mary.

THE ROSARY

There are twenty mysteries of the life of Jesus that we meditate on when praying the Rosary: five Joyful Mysteries, five Luminous Mysteries, five Sorrowful Mysteries, and five Glorious Mysteries.

MYSTERIES OF THE ROSARY

Joyful Mysteries

1. The Annunciation
2. The Visitation
3. The Birth of Our Lord
4. The Presentation of Jesus in the Temple
5. The Finding of Jesus in the Temple

Luminous Mysteries

1. The Baptism of Jesus
2. Jesus Reveals Himself in the Miracle at Cana
3. Jesus Proclaims the Good News of the Kingdom of God
4. The Transfiguration of Jesus
5. The Institution of the Eucharist

Sorrowful Mysteries

1. The Agony of Jesus in the Garden
2. The Scourging at the Pillar
3. The Crowning of Thorns
4. The Carrying of the Cross
5. The Crucifixion

 Glorious Mysteries

1. The Resurrection of Jesus
2. The Ascension of Jesus into Heaven
3. The Descent of the Holy Spirit on the Apostles (Pentecost)
4. The Assumption of Mary into Heaven
5. The Crowning of Mary as Queen of Heaven

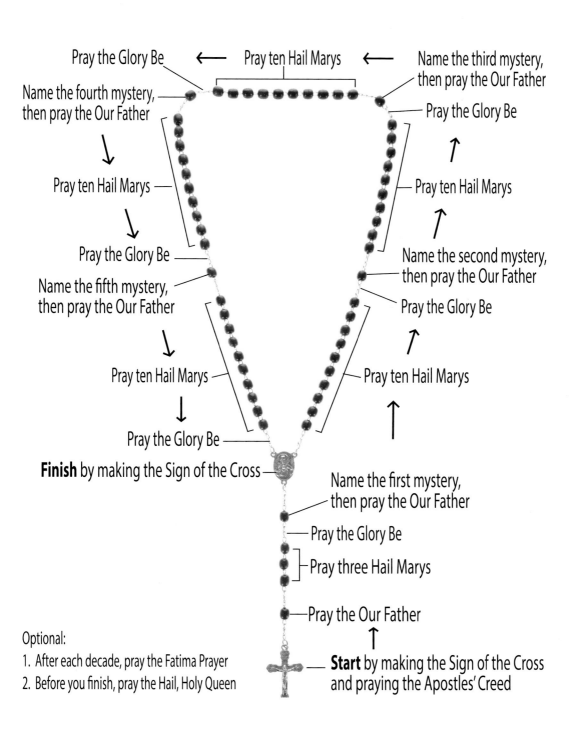

Pray the Glory Be ← Pray ten Hail Marys ← Name the third mystery, then pray the Our Father

Name the fourth mystery, then pray the Our Father

Pray the Glory Be

Pray ten Hail Marys

Pray ten Hail Marys

Pray the Glory Be

Name the fifth mystery, then pray the Our Father

Name the second mystery, then pray the Our Father

Pray the Glory Be

Pray ten Hail Marys

Pray ten Hail Marys

Pray the Glory Be

Finish by making the Sign of the Cross

Name the first mystery, then pray the Our Father

Pray the Glory Be

Pray three Hail Marys

Pray the Our Father

Optional:
1. After each decade, pray the Fatima Prayer
2. Before you finish, pray the Hail, Holy Queen

Start by making the Sign of the Cross and praying the Apostles' Creed

List of Prayers and Practices

L

M

N

O

P

R

S

T

W